I Know Who I Am:

Declarations from the Word to Set You Free

LADY HELENA BARNES

Book Description

This book, I Know Who I Am, is an inspirational book of declarations, focused on making the word of God a vital component of daily success in life. Many Christians do not embrace the entire Bible, or believe it "to the very last bit." Sometimes, we think some aspects of the Scriptures can work for us, and other parts are archaic or relate best to other people. However, the truth of the matter is that the word of God is life. It is true. It is authentic. It is relevant; it is powerful. And it is not seasonal but is supposed to be a consistent guide to our everyday victory. And above all, it is for all mankind: young or old, rich or poor, white or black, and everyone that has breath.

The word of God, which is the Bible, is a sacred book. And just like any conventional manual, we are to use the Bible as a tool to redirect us back on track. We need the Bible to deliver us from any misconceptions of who we have truly been created to be. Daily confession of the word of God boosts our confidence, helps us diffuse lies from the enemy about who we truly are in Christ, and will help us stay on track.

This book is designed to make the reader know that life and death are in the power of the tongue of the believer and proper use of it breeds life and advancement. Silence gives the enemy an upper hand. Choose life and live it to the fullest by engaging this book. Remember, the saying goes, "a closed mouth is a closed destiny."

Let the truth of God's word set you free.

Copyright © 2019 Helena Barnes. All rights reserved. Published 2019.

PurposeHouse Publishing, Columbia, Maryland

ISBN-13: 978-0-9963647-3-7

No part of this publication may be reproduced or distributed in any form or by any means, or stored in a database or retrieval system, without the prior written permission of the publisher. Email requests for permission to ministeringpurpose@gmail.com.

Unless otherwise indicated, all scriptural quotations are from the King James Version of the Bible, which is in the public domain.

Scripture from the American Standard Version (ASV), public domain

Scripture from Amplified Bible (AMP, Copyright © 1987 by the Lockman Foundation. (www.Lockman.org))

American Bible Classic Edition (AMPC, Copyright © by the Lockman Foundation. (www.Lockman.org))

Scripture from the Contemporary English Version (CEV), Copyright © 1995 by American Bible Society

Complete Jewish Bible (CJB), Copyright © 1998 by David H. Stern.

English Standard Version (ESV), Copyright © 2001 by Crossway, a publishing ministry of Good News Publishers.

Scripture from the Living Bible (TLB), copyright © 1971 by Tyndale House Foundation, Used by permission of Tyndale House Publishers Inc., Carol Stream, Illinois 60188. All rights reserved.

Scripture from the Message Bible (MSG), Copyright © 1993, 1994, 1995, 1996, 2000, 2001, 2002 by Eugene H. Peterson, All rights reserved

Scripture from the New International Version (NIV), Copyright © 1973, 1978, 1984 by Biblica.

Scripture from New King James Version (NKJV), Copyright © 1982 by Thomas Nelson, Inc., All rights reserved.

Scripture from the New Life Version (NLV), Copyright © 1969 by Christian Literature International.

Scripture from the New Living Translation (NLT), Copyright © 1996, 2004 by Tyndale Charitable Trust.

Scripture from the Wycliffe Bible (WYC), copyright © 2001 by Terence P. Noble.

Dedication

I dedicate this book to my immediate family. First, to my husband, my first, true love--the one I have grown to call and have known as a true and genuine friend. You have taught me so many things that have made me the beautiful woman that is by your side today.

From the beginning, our connection changed the trajectory of my life. I was a girl who had given up, but your daily words of encouragement revived me. Today, I am alive with you by my side. Your motivation and encouragement are invaluable. They have caused me to believe in myself and my God-given dreams. For that, I am eternally grateful.

Second, to my sons Caleb, Jesse, Aaron, and Israel Barnes, you bring me so much joy, and the willingness to see each new day with strength and power. I see how my God is blessing you all and grooming you, and I never want to miss a day of it. By the grace of God, I promise to be there until the very end of it all.

You all have unique characteristics, and I love each one of you dearly. May the good Lord shield, cover, and protect you daily. Thank you all for being my cheerleaders in everything I do. You were there for me in my first journey of writing *I Love Me*, and you still supported me with the second book as well. You all are my biggest fans, and Mum is proud of you all. Thank you Barnes boys!

Acknowledgements

I give all glory to God, my Heavenly Father, who placed this vision inside of me as a sequel to the first book, *I Love Me*, to bring hope and awaken his children from slumber and deception. Many have fallen along the wayside and out of faith; they have lost their identity and feel hopeless. But I give God praise for choosing me as a conduit to bring their love, passion, and focus back to Him.

I am proclaiming that life's circumstances must not define us. Only His unadulterated Word should bring transformation to our lives and be the yardstick for our walk with him. Confession of God's word brings possession!

Bishop Kibby Otoo, my spiritual and adopted father, words cannot describe how much I appreciate and cherish you. Right from the very first time you came into my life, you have fought tooth and nail through strategic prayers, and in all forms to keep me here on earth. As your daughter, you would do anything for me. You have taught me how to pray and do ministry, and what you continue to do for me is invaluable. I am so grateful that God made this connection and declare it will never be altered, in Jesus' name. On behalf of my husband and our boys, I say a big thank you, and I pray you increase in strength and power daily.

To a sister, a friend, and a woman of God, First Lady Elsie Otoo, I want to say a big thank you to you for being a true sister. You saw in me what I did not see and gave me a chance to do ministry. And now, I have the opportunity to share this devotional with the world and be a blessing to many. I will always cherish you.

To a great mother and mentor, Pastor Lenita Reeves, I want to pour out my sincere gratitude to you for always making yourself available to help and coach and bring the best out of people. Being a seasoned author yourself, your counsel helped me through my first book. The countless hours we both spent going through this journey has been nothing but pure love and dedication for a daughter in Christ.

To my spiritual daughters Beverly Boachie and Stacy Danquah who were my cheerleaders for this particular book, you kept tabs on me weekly, made sure I was meeting deadlines, and read the draft periodically to help me stay on point. And sometimes, even haunted me by sending text messages to get to work. I appreciate your love and motivation every step of the way. Writing this book has been a journey but a great success! History has been made again! I love you both dearly.

Contents

Foreword, 13
Introduction, 15

Section 1: Understanding the Power of Studying and Speaking the Word

Chapter 1: Satanic Strategies to Keep Us from Knowing Our True Identity, 17
Chapter 2: Finding True Identity Through the Word of God and Prayer, 21
Chapter 3: The Importance of Keeping the Word of God Alive In You Daily, 23
Chapter 4: Effective Prayer and Declarations, 27

Section 2: Releasing God's Truth: Declarations for 8 Areas of Life

Chapter 5: Declarations for Our Identity as Children of God, 33
Chapter 6: Declarations for Soul Winning, 39
Chapter 7: Declarations for Finances, 45
Chapter 8: Declarations for Marriage, 49
Chapter 9: Declarations for Health, 53
Chapter 10: Declarations for Career/Business, 57
Chapter 11: Declarations for Ministry, 61
Chapter 12: Declarations for Children, 65

Appendix 1: The Ten Commandments, 71
Appendix 2: The Beatitudes, 75

Foreword

Have you checked your environment today? Look closely, and you'll likely find a cell phone, laptop, tablet, radio, and television all within your reach. This is the world as we know it today. We are so connected (technologically speaking) but not connected to what matters most. Media, marketing, and mobile phones continuously bombard us. Each day, our brains filter thousands of messages contrary to the word of God; most of which we carry with us on something called a *smartphone*. But how smart is that?

In this book, Helena Barnes reminds us that the word of God is the essential daily dose of information we need. She tells us that it is alive and powerful. It's so powerful it drowns the voices that cause us to question our identity and the integrity of God's promises. But I expect that from Lady Helena. She has stayed faithful to her *I Love Me* mandate, pointing readers to the source of their true identity—the word of God.

This time, she takes another step. Instead of devotionals, this book includes scriptures and declarations for eight critical areas of life. Not only are readers encouraged to consume the word but also speak it, declaring their covenant rights in the areas of identity, soul-winning, finances, marriage, health, career/business, ministry, and children.

In this day and age, we desperately need to return to the Scriptures, which are a sure word of prophecy and anchor for our souls. I encourage everyone to read this book and speak what's in it, for this is what Lady Helena helps us to do throughout its pages—read the word and speak it.

Rev. Lenita Reeves, Senior Pastor, Action Chapel Baltimore

Introduction

Throughout a person's life, individual relationships, experiences, culture, media, and the world around them can influence their identity. And sometimes, many are never able to say what their true identity is. Some even check out of this world without having full knowledge of who they are, and what they are called to do. God created us, and undoubtedly, He had a perfect image in mind for everyone. We can only see our true image by the connection we have with him, and inevitably, the love that we have for his word. That connection will gradually etch out our true identity and give us dominion over all obstacles in life. The word of the Lord declares, "And ye shall know the truth, and the truth shall make you free" (John 8:31-32 KJV). And John 15:7 says, "If ye abide in me, and my words abide in you, ye shall ask what ye will, and it shall be done unto you."

We need to be in love with the word of God, so at least we can know his stance on life's issues and also receive answers to our prayer requests. As believers, we also ought to know that not every prayer request gets answered, especially if it does not align with God's word. There are conditions attached to our asking from the Lord. And one of them is simply abiding in the word of God. Absolute freedom and victory are anchored in the word of truth.

Some mountains we face in life are because of our ignorance of the truths in the Bible, which is God's wisdom to us. The Bible helps guide and walk us through this life as victors and not victims. Most of the patriarchs and matriarchs we know, or have heard about, obtained recognition and worked miracles because they gave their all to studying of the word of God. They showed themselves approved by rightly dividing the word of truth, just as the scripture admonishes us to do.

2 Timothy 2:15 says, "Study to show thyself approved unto God, a workman that needeth not to be ashamed, rightly dividing the word of truth." The truth is, many of us have allowed the world to tell us who we are. When instead, we should let our Creator reveal our true identity through an authentic relationship with him. God gave everything he created identity. The enemy is trying to erase our identity by severing our relationship with our maker. As a result, we do not know what he says about us, let alone to find and walk in our true identity. There is a daily, spiritual war going on over our identity. The war is all in an attempt to derail us from purpose, cause us to believe lies about ourselves, sabotage our destinies, or get manipulated to make declarations over ourselves that do not reflect God's original plan for us.

One of the things the enemy, who is Satan, does best is to mislead, distort, and destroy. The enemy plans to get back at God, and if distorts and destroys what God has invested so much in, then he has succeeded in hurting God (by hurting God's children).

Chapter 1: Satanic Strategies to Keep Us from Knowing Our True Identity

Our number one enemy, the devil, moves around like a roaring lion looking for whom he may devour. Satan has several strategies he uses to confuse and blind Christians or children of God from knowing who they are, coming into a full understanding of their original identity. His strategies are so ruthless, and he can use any willing vessel to execute his agenda over our lives and destinies. The word of God tells us the assignment of the enemy–Satan. It is to steal, to kill, and to destroy. Most of us live in denial, thinking that because we are children of the King of Kings, the enemy cannot plan our demise. The enemy will do everything to have us walk in deception, and believe what people say about us, which is contrary to what our maker thinks about us. He wants to make us self-destructive, and feel inferior and less valuable all in a ploy to destroy and fight our identity. That's his aim, and he is very relentless about it.

Strategy 1: *Opinions of other people*

Our parents, peers, spouses, colleagues, enemies, and friends alike may have said things about us throughout our life journey. Not everything said may be true, but most of the times, they say things due to their perception of us. Our inadequacies may have shaped their opinion. Or errors we made due to bad decisions, or their merely being mean (or just trying to make us be like them and not what God wants us to be).

People are entitled to their own opinions, but they did not create us. We must not allow our lives to come to a standstill because of what an ordinary person is saying about us. The best way to fight this evil strategy against our identity is to surrender our lives completely to God. Obviously, the enemy's power is nothing to compare with our Heavenly Father, but winning this attack is all predicated on whose side you are. When we are committed to God, we will obey his word, and hold on to what his word says about who we are in him. Constant focus on his word will free our minds from negativity, increase our faith, and cause us to know who we truly are in Christ.

Strategy 2: *Pain / Offense*

Offenses have a way of making us bitter, resentful, and hateful. As a result, we shut people out, and this is a trusted tool the enemy can use against us to miss what God has called us to be. Sometimes, we make vows to ourselves never to be like our parents due to past situations, and we instead end up being like them. And we may become even worse than our parents because we did not allow the pain to be healed.

Most of the time, we do not acknowledge the fact that we are offended, but the healing process will begin by first knowing and accepting that there is an offense. We must acknowledge the pain in our heart before we can proceed to the next stage of dealing with it. The number one recommendation to deal with offense and pain is forgiveness.

We can get so caught up in the offense that we end up forgetting people and becoming something else. The next thing is, we must be willing to work through the process of healing. Reading God's word and being flexible for the Holy Spirit to minister to us is another way of being free from offense. Offense can take someone to such a deep place that only the intervention of the power of the Holy Ghost, who will permeate deep into the crevices of the heart, will bring total healing. Counseling may not do it, fellowship may not, money may not, but allowing God to take over brings total freedom and peace, and makes us heaven bound. It is often said that hurt people hurt other people. We must learn to let go and let God and the Holy Spirit have a free course in our lives.

Strategy 3: *Social Media*

There is so much that goes on these days on social media. People are doing things, saying things, engaging in things, and bullying. These things can destroy a person's image, defame someone, and even cause someone to take their own life. Social media has also become a competition ground where people measure themselves according to unrealistic standards. This can lead to depression, which sometimes graduates to self-imposed curses and death.

Shame, guilt, confusion, un-forgiveness, and low self-worth are all from the devil so he can steal our identity. But God says in his word that he did not come to condemn the world but to save it.

The best way to avoid being a victim on social

media is by either minimizing our visits and postings or completely deleting our account if need be. Many use it for business, and I think it should be professional and solely business. We should never look at people and their images and feel inferior or have depression because, by our judgment, they are special and better looking. We may not know what they are dealing with physically, spiritually, martially, economically, and socially. A mere picture posted can be a charade, covering a lot of hidden personal issues. We should know who Christ says we are in him and not compare or compete with people online. We ought to be careful and discerning enough about who we accept as friends because what they do, and how they behave can reflect either negatively or positively on us. Everything we do in this life requires great wisdom. I believe we can fight evil with good by having a positive counter approach to insinuations, insults, and sabotages without having to be like what we abhor.

Chapter 2: Finding True Identity Through the Word of God and Prayer

When we have God, we can boldly say we have more than enough. In this day and age, we do not need just casual prayers. We ought to be a people at the cutting edge of strong and powerful prayers to dislodge and destroy satanic forces that relentlessly bombard the children of God. It is always a life and death situation. There is power in our tongues, and we have the propensity to create life with it or bring about death. Speak life over your identity. We must make a conscious effort to speak life over our lives and situations to see a complete turnaround.

It will take prayers and a whole lot of it to take this war to the enemy's gate. Our effectual and fervent prayers can stop Satan from winning over the souls of Gods people. Constant declarations on topical issues over our identity, family, children, health, finances, education, carrier, business, ministry and many more will frustrate the devices and the tokens of the enemy and will give us victory daily. Ignorance and prayerlessness is a luxury we as Christians can never afford. We must let prayer be our portion, our pastime, our passion, and must be intentional in this dispensation we are in. Our God is well able to perform and do exceedingly abundantly, far above all that we ask and think of, and what he has promised us in his word.

We are powerful creations of God. If the adversary can have us believe otherwise, then we will always operate below standard, and settle for less. We will live beneath the benefits of our true identity. He created us to rule, have dominion, and take charge (Genesis 1:26-28 KJV). However, if only we accustom ourselves to what our creator has said, we can effectively prevail over situations and obstacles in life. We can enforce what he said through prayer concerning any particular matter. Every issue in life has a solution or wisdom nugget in the word of God to bring about peace and victory. His word declares, "My people are destroyed for lack of knowledge: because thou hast rejected knowledge, I will also reject thee, that thou shalt be no priest to me: seeing thou hast forgotten the law of thy God, I will also forget thy children" (Hosea 4:6 KJV). Make a commitment to study the word and find out who God says you are. Continually confess that you were created to rule, dominate, and take charge (Genesis 1:26-28).

Chapter 3: The Importance of Keeping the Word of God Alive In You Daily

The passage, Joshua 1:8 declares, "This book of the law shall not depart out of thy mouth; but thou shalt meditate therein day and night, that thou mayest observe to do according to all that is written therein: for then thou shalt make thy way prosperous, and then thou shalt have good success."

This scripture makes it very clear that God wants to prosper us and make us successful. But that power has been given to us and can only be activated through our daily devotion and commitment to his word.

The word of God reveals to us the mind of God and what his will is for us. The passage, 2 Timothy 3:16-17 says, "All scripture is given by inspiration of God, and is profitable for doctrine, for reproof, for correction, for instruction in righteousness, that the man of God may be complete thoroughly equipped for every good work."

Here are four reasons why you must keep the word of God alive in you daily.

1. His word is Infallible. The word of God is inerrant and perfect.
    - Every word of God is pure: he is a shield unto them that put their trust in him. Add thou not unto his words, lest he reprove thee, and thou be found a liar (Proverbs 30:5-6KJV).
    - This scripture admonishes us to receive the word of God just as it is presented because of its purity.

2. His word will bring to pass what it was originally sent forth to do.
   - So shall my word be that goeth forth out of my mouth: it shall not return unto me void, but it shall accomplish that which I please, and it shall prosper in the thing whereto I sent it (Isaiah 55:11 KJV)
   - This scripture endorses the authenticity of God's word. It makes us know that God is not a liar, and we are assured hope and victory if we hold fast to his word and anything it has declared.

3. His word is very dependable.
   - Forever, O Lord, thy word is settled in heaven (Psalm 119:89 KJV)
   - God's word is very powerful, and it carries absolute authority. Therefore, when we indulge in his word, that spirit of power and authority is imparted to us to decree and declare things into existence. The word also helps us deal with the forces of darkness. These forces are determined to keep us under and never above.

4. His word is very efficient and adequate for our daily needs.
   - All scripture is given by inspiration of God, and is profitable for doctrine, for reproof, for correction, for instruction in righteousness: That the man of God may be perfect, thoroughly

furnished unto all good works (2 Timothy 3:16-17 KJV).

The word of God brings so much assurance. When we learn to study it daily, we can know what he is saying regarding issues and challenges for that day, which will help us avoid unnecessary errors and destiny altering mistakes. Keep the word of God alive inside you daily.

Chapter 4: Effective Prayers and Declarations

My spiritual "grandfather," Archbishop Nicolas Duncan-Williams, says that prayer is:
- The vehicle that carries the predetermined counsel of God to his children
- The means to enforce the judicial determination of heaven from eternity into time
- The womb that carries the ordinances of Elohim to execute and superimpose them over the earth realm, and the systems of this world

Archbishop says that heaven is limited to what it can do over this earth without prayer. Until prayer goes up, heaven can do nothing for humanity. One of the Christian generals and patriarchs by the name of John Wesley says, "God can do nothing for humanity until somebody prays."

Now, how do we pray effective prayers and hold God to his promises? First of all, by having a relationship with our heavenly father, subsequently being hungry for his word, and then, avoiding the temptation to pray amiss. The Bible says that God's words will never return void. So shall my word be that goeth forth out of my mouth: it shall not return unto me void, but it shall accomplish that which I please, and it shall prosper in the thing whereto I sent it (Isaiah 55:11 KJV).

It is important to understand that when God declares something, it will accomplish what he pleases. You must also declare the word of God. You must make declarations.

Declarations

In layman's terms, to declare is just to speak forth, to announce, to utter, to proclaim, to affirm, and to avow. Words are very powerful. One of the greatest gifts God gave us human beings is our vocal cords and the ability to speak and to interact. We do sometimes take it for granted. We do not value what we have until it is taken from us. It is the will of God that we speak his promises back to him and not be quiet or just internalize it. A lot of us find it difficult to speak out his words to avert the wickedness of the enemy over our lives, but it is so easy and second nature to many to speak and announce negative, evil, disappointment, pain, sickness, and many more things that do not bring God glory.

Here are four reasons you must make declarations that are in line with and backed by the word of God.

1. Declarations generate life.

The tongue has the power of life and death, and those who love it will eat its fruit (Proverbs 18:21 NIV). God has given us a powerful weapon, which is the tongue, which also has the ability to release life to dead, hopeless, and condemned situations. It is not easy to make positive declarations because our adversary knows the weight and damage it can cause to his kingdom. So as long as we are mute and silent, he is great. We rather speak according to what we feel, experience, and endure. This is not of God. We must stand upon His word, declare His mind concerning our situation, and experience change by that act of faith. Be intentional about your speaking and make utterances or declarations that carry life and not death.

2. Declarations allow us to experience Jesus's victory in our lives.

For by thy words thou shalt be justified, and by thy words thou shalt be condemned (Proverbs 18:21 NIV). Our words can either bring limitations to our lives or a blessing to us. We shall eat the fruit of what we declare; so therefore, we need to be mindful what we allow to come out of our mouths. We will be judged by it. There is nothing more powerful than us aligning our pronouncements or declarations with the word of God.

3. Declarations expedite our access to our Land of promise.

We know from his word in Joshua 1:8 that the scriptures should never depart from our mouths. As we meditate upon the word of God, we must keep it on our lips to defuse the power of negative pronouncements or unfavorable situations. When we are sick, we need to declare that we are strong, because his word declares that when we are weak, then we are strong. His strength is perfect in our weakness. His word says the poor should declare that they are rich, and the barren that they are fruitful all because the word of God is powerful. It can overturn the evil force behind issues and occurrences that do not bring God glory.

4. Declarations give us confidence and hope to bring invisible things into the realm of visibility/manifestation.

As it is written, I have made thee a father of many nations before him whom he believed, even God, who quickeneth the dead, and calleth those things, which be not as though they were (Romans 4:17 KJV). Our words do create. We carry the same creative power that brought about the creation because we have Christ, the creator in us. And we can do even more than he did if only we believe we have what it takes. Declarations, whether they be evil or good, (what we keep on our mouths constantly) are what will manifest. Therefore, speak well and choose life!

Section 2: Releasing God's Truth: Declarations for 8 Areas of Life

1. Our Identity as Children of God
2. Soul Winning
3. Finances
4. Marriage
5. Health
6. Career/Business
7. Ministry
8. Children

Chapter 5: Declarations for Our Identity as Children of God

Kingdom Truths Concerning Our Identity and Prayer Declarations

Author and psychologist David Benner defines identity as "who we experience ourselves to be; the 'I' each of us carries within." The truth in his book, *The Gift of Being Yourself,* states that a lot of people identify themselves through their jobs, financial status, successes, grades, appearance, and what other people say about them. But it is crucial to know that our true identity is not in material things but found in Christ. Many Christians do not find contentment in themselves and are very confused about who they truly are. The initial intent of God for us was for us to reflect his glory here on earth and anything outside of that will not bring gratification to God but to ourselves. There will never be actual fulfillment outside of God. We can know who we are by building and staying in a relationship with our Heavenly Father, and knowing what his word says about us and who he made us to be.

His Word says...
So God created human beings in his own image. In the image of God he created them; male and female he created them (Genesis 1:27 NLT).

Now You Declare
I decree and declare that I am created in the image and likeness of God. Therefore, I am unique among all of God's creation. He took his time to make me while he called all other things into existence. I have the resemblance of God. Mentally, I will reflect his intellect and wisdom. Morally, I will live a pure and holy life. Socially, I will love others just as God loves them. I will not devalue myself, and I vow to honor God with my life and serve him till eternity. I know the truth, and I will allow it to set me free today.

His Word says...
Knowing this, that our old man is crucified with him, that the body of sin might be destroyed, that henceforth we should not serve sin (Romans 6:6 KJV).

Now You Declare
I decree and declare I am a new creation, old things are passed away, and I decide this day to separate myself from sin. Holy Spirit, help me overcome sin completely and live a holy and consecrated life unto God. My old self is crucified with Christ daily, and I will be a role model for my generation.

His Word says...
For in Christ lives all the fullness of God in a human body. So you also are complete through your union with Christ, who is the head over every ruler and authority (Colossians 2:9-10 NLT).

Now You Declare
I decree and declare that I am not empty. I am a complete human being, and I am filled up in the fullness of God. I will grow in the measure of the stature of the fullness of Christ. I commit myself this day to stay focused on Christ and will not allow anything to derail me or destroy my faith. I have been given completeness and fullness in Christ; therefore, I will not let philosophies and traditions deceive me. I know the truth, and I will allow it to set me free today.

His Word says...
But you are a chosen people, a royal priesthood, a holy nation, God's special possession, that you may declare the praises of him who called you out of darkness into his wonderful light (1 Peter 2:9 NIV).

Now You Declare
I decree and declare that I am chosen by God. I am royalty, a holy nation, and I am his special possession. I am a child of God, called into his marvelous light, and I have nothing to do with darkness. My past is all forgiven, and I am new in Christ. I am cleansed from sin by the blood of Jesus Christ and sanctified internally by the Holy Spirit of God. I will no longer live in guilt, shame, depression, anger, and have low self-esteem because Christ has paid the price for me. I know the truth, and I will allow it to set me free today.

His Word says...
Before I formed thee in the belly I knew thee; and before

thou camest forth out of the womb I sanctified thee, and I ordained thee a prophet unto the nations (Jeremiah 1:5 KJV).

Now You Declare
I decree and declare that I am not a surprise to my creator. He knew my substance before he formed me in my mother's belly. I am not useless before God. He has a plan for my life and has sanctified me to a special office in his kingdom. I will this day allow myself to go through the pruning, the process, and the training, and when I am all ready, my life will make sense and will be beautiful in God's glory. I know the truth, and I will allow it to set me free today.

His word says...
Behold, what manner of love the Father hath bestowed upon us, that we should be called the sons of God: therefore the world knoweth us not, because it knew him not. Beloved, now are we the sons of God, and it doth not yet appear what we shall be: (1 John 3:1-2 KJV)

Now you declare
I decree and declare that God is my father. I have been chosen and adopted through Christ as his own. I am honored and privileged to be called his child. Having God as my father gives me hope for my future. I know he will always be on my side. Many do not know him because they have not been. I decree today that I will make him known, and I will continually testify of his goodness. I know the truth, and I will allow it to set me

free today.

His word says...
If ye then be risen with Christ, seek those things which are above, where Christ sitteth on the right hand of God. Set your affection on things above, not on things on the earth. For ye are dead, and your life is hid with Christ in God (Colossians 3:1-3 KJV).

Now you declare
I decree and declare that my identity is in Christ Jesus. Therefore, I will set my mind on spiritual matters and things above and not things of the earth. I will let kingdom affairs concern and motivate me more. Issues of life will not derail me from my purpose and assignment here on earth. I will be about my father's business. I decide this day to be true to Christ always; so my glory, honor, and reward will not be circumvented. I know the truth, and I will allow it to set me free today.

His word says...
Blessed be the God and Father of our Lord Jesus Christ, who hath blessed us with all spiritual blessings in heavenly places in Christ: According as he hath chosen us in him before the foundation of the world, that we should be holy and without blame before him in love: Having predestinated us unto the adoption of children by Jesus Christ to himself, according to the good pleasure of his will (Ephesians 1:3-5 KJV).

Now you declare
I decree and declare today that I am blessed and favored

by the Lord in all spiritual blessings. I know this for sure because I am in Christ Jesus. I am chosen, adopted, redeemed, forgiven, loved, and accepted. Lord, by your grace, I will live a holy and blameless life. I have strength and divine power to overcome all forms of challenges that will cause me to compromise my salvation. My focus is on you, Lord, and I have faith that you will see me through every step of the way. I know the truth, and I will allow it to set me free today.

Chapter 6: Declarations for Soul-Winning

Kingdom truths concerning Soul Winning and Prayer Declarations

Soul-winning is an essential subject when it comes to Christianity, and our walk with Christ Jesus. As children of God, we ought to avail ourselves to be instruments in the hands of God to use us to bring precious and lost souls back to the Kingdom. Soul-winning should be the number one passion of every believer. We should be enthused to share our experiences, our breakthroughs, our testimonies, and our faith. It is a command from God to win souls. Anyone who wins souls for God is considered wise.

His Word Says...
And Jesus came and spake unto them, saying, All power is given unto me in heaven and in earth. Go ye therefore, and teach all nations, baptizing them in the name of the Father, and of the Son, and of the Holy Ghost: Teaching them to observe all things whatsoever I have commanded you: and, lo, I am with you always, even unto the end of the world. Amen (Matthew 28:18-20 KJV).

Now You Declare
I decree and declare that I have received Jesus Christ as my Lord and personal savior. He lives in me and I in Him. I have been blessed since I came to the saving knowledge of Christ, and I cannot keep this fantastic testimony to myself. I will go to the nations, and the

ends of the world to proclaim His goodness towards me. I shall not be afraid of the gospel of Jesus Christ. I will tell it on the mountaintops, in the valleys and everywhere, what the Lord has done for me. I will not operate in my own power and strength, but the power that has been given to me from above. I know the truth, and I will allow it to set me free today.

His Word Says ...
And so also were James and John, sons of Zebedee, who were partners with Simon. And Jesus said to Simon, "Do not fear, from now on you will be catching men (Luke 5:10
KJV).

Now You Declare
I decree and declare today that I am found and I am no longer lost in the world. I am in Christ; therefore, I will identify my purpose in life. I shall no longer be aimless and confused. One of my purposes is to reach out to the lost souls and bring them to Christ. I receive the grace and anointing for this assignment, and I cast out all fears from my life this day and forevermore. I know the truth, and I will allow it to set me free today.

His Word Says
For though I am free from all men, I have made myself a slave to all, so that I may win more (1 Corinthians 9:19 KJV).

Now You Declare
I decree and declare today that I am free! The spirit of bondage is broken off my life. I am no longer a slave to men because I belong to God. I shall continue to walk in this freedom and not permit anything to enslave me ever again, not sin, sex, drugs, deception, or abuse from men. My new lifestyle will be a testament to God's goodness towards me and will cause many to be won to the Lord. My life shall not drive people away from God, but it will be admirable and an example of how a Christian should live. I know the truth, and I will allow it to set me free today.

His Word Says...
To the Jews I became as a Jew, so that I might win Jews; to those who are under the Law, as under the Law though not being myself under the Law, so that I might win those who are under the Law (1 Corinthians 9:20 KJV)

Now You Declare
I decree and declare that I will not be judgmental towards people. It is just by the grace of God that I am where I am today. I pray today that God will use me as a vessel to be able to reach all that will be reachable. The poor, the homeless, the rejected, the hopeless, the abandoned, the depressed, the lost, the blind, from all walks of life, I will be able to relate with them and win them to Christ. I humble myself this day for God mighty desire for lost souls to be made manifest. I know the truth, and I will allow it to set me free today.

His Word Says ...
Those who have insight will shine brightly like the brightness of the expanse of heaven, and those who lead the many to righteousness, like the stars forever and ever (Daniel 12:3 NASB)

Now You Declare
I decree and declare that I am godly and wise. My life will shine brightly each day like the brightness of the expanse of heaven. God's greatness, power, and uniqueness will rest upon me. My lifestyle and testimonies will influence others to come to the saving knowledge of Christ. Because I follow Jesus, and his light reflects in me, my path will shine brighter and brighter each day, and through that, lost souls will also find their way to Jesus, the author, and finisher of our faith. I know the truth, and I will allow it to set me free today.

His word says...
But sanctify the Lord God in your hearts: and be ready always to give an answer to every man that asketh you a reason of the hope that is in you with meekness and fear (1 Peter 3:15 KJV).

Now you declare
I decree and declare today that I will revere the Lord at all times, both inwardly and outwardly. I shall not be ashamed of the source of my strength. He has done so much for me, and I shall share my testimony with the whole world. It is in my sharing and appreciation that I get more blessed. I shall not be a judge, I will not

accuse, I will not point fingers, I will not be prideful or boastful, but I will share the love of God with humility to all men. I know the truth, and I will allow it to set me free today.

His Word says...

The fruit of the righteous [is] a tree of life; and he that winneth souls [is] wise (Proverbs 11:30 KJV)

Now you declare

I decree and declare that I am righteous and fruitful. My fruit is a tree of life. I will be intentional about my actions and dealings with whoever comes my way because I am an ambassador of Christ. My assignment is to win many to the Kingdom of God. He calls me wise when I win souls. I know the truth, and I will allow it to set me free today.

His word says...

Ye have not chosen me, but I have chosen you, and ordained you, that ye should go and bring forth fruit, and [that] your fruit should remain: that whatsoever ye shall ask of the Father in my name, he may give it you (John 15:16 KJV).

Now you declare

I decree and declare today that I am chosen. I did not choose myself, but my Heavenly Father did. I have been divinely ordained and given the mandate to go into the world to bring forth fruit, preaching the gospel to the lost souls. None of my fruit shall backslide but will be firmly grounded and shall remain in the house of the Lord. My obedience will cause me to have favor from God, and whatsoever I ask the Father in the name of Jesus I will receive. I know the truth, and I will allow it to set me free today.

His word says...
That if thou shalt confess with thy mouth the Lord Jesus, and shalt believe in thine heart that God hath raised him from the dead, thou shalt be saved (Romans 10:9 KJV).

Now you declare
I decree and declare today that with my mouth, I shall confess Jesus as my Lord and savior. I accept with my heart that God raised Him from the dead, so I shall be saved. For with my heart, I believe unto righteousness, and with my mouth confession shall be made unto salvation. Because I believe, I shall not be ashamed. He is "my everything" and my ever-present help in times of trouble. I know the truth, and I will allow it to set me free today.

Chapter 7: Declarations for Finances

Kingdom truths concerning Finances and Prayer Declarations

One of the greatest challenges that believers encounter in life is financial lack. The enemy has managed to sell us a lie. And many cannot rise above that lie but work around it and settle for crumbs or with poverty. Some find it very hard to appropriate the biblical principles for financial freedom. The word of God brings life to our spirit, our relationships, and our finances. The good Lord has plans to prosper his children. He did not bring us into this world to abandon us. There are principles and promises in his wisdom book that show us what to do to be financially empowered, to be above only and not beneath. Knowing what the truth is and living by it will bring peace in our finances and make us a blessing to many generations.

His words says...
And though you started with little, you will end with much. (Job 8:7 NLT)
Though thy beginning was small, yet thy latter end should greatly increase. (Job 8:7 KJV)

Now you declare
I decree and declare today that I am not poor. I am rich. I am first spirit before natural. My spiritual DNA is of one who is never poor, who never lacks, or ever in need. My provision comes from the one who owns the cattle on a thousand hills. He became poor by virtue of his

crucifixion so I will become rich. I will not despise my small beginnings for my Father is working it all out for my good. Though my present state may be little, my expectation of a greater end shall not be cut off. My Father shall enlarge my territory and make me a blessing to many. I know the truth, and I will allow it to set me free.

His word says...
But my God shall supply all your need according to his riches in glory by Christ Jesus. (Philippians 4:19 KJV)

Now you declare
I decree and declare that I have no lack! My source is not my job, my family, my friends, or my businesses. But my source and daily supply come from my maker, the great provider. He has promised never to leave me nor forsake me. He is rich! As his child, I pronounce today that I am a part of his dynasty. Anything I need that will bring him glory is hereby supplied in Jesus name! I confess today that I shall never lack another day in my life, in Jesus name. I know the truth, and I will allow it to set me free.

His word says...
The blessing of the Lord makes a person rich, and he adds no sorrow with it. (Proverbs 10:22 NLT)

Now You Declare
I decree and declare that I am blessed of the Lord! His blessings upon my life shall make me rich and not poor. Everything I do shall prosper and not fail. I shall see

increase and overflow in my life. In the morning, I am blessed, in the noonday, I am blessed, and in the evening, I will remain blessed. Everything I possess that has suffered attacks from the cankerworm or caterpillar shall resurrect again in Jesus name. I rebuke cycles of indebtedness, lack, bankruptcy, pain, frustrations, borrowing, loaning, and renting. I confess today that I have more than enough, I will lend and not borrow, and I will own and not rent. May the blood of Jesus surround all I have so I experience no sorrow. I know the truth, and I will allow it to set me free.

His word says...
He that trusteth in his riches shall fall: but
the righteous shall flourish as a branch (Proverbs 11:28 KJV)

Now You Declare
I decree and declare that I am blessed and highly favored of the Lord. I confess that I am a child of God, and I am born again. Everything I have, I obtained from the Lord. He has made me a steward of everything and a possessor of nothing. I will always depend on my divine provider, and he shall supply all my needs according to his riches through Christ Jesus. My security is not in my material wealth, but my trust shall forever be in the Lord my God, who knows my uprising and my downsitting. I confess today that I shall flourish in every endeavor of my life. Nothing I lay my hands to do will fall because I surrender all to God, the author and finisher of my faith. I know the truth, and I will allow it to set me free.

His word says...
The LORD shall open unto thee
his good treasure, the heaven to give the rain unto
thy land in his season, and to bless all the work of
thine hand: and thou shalt lend unto many nations, and
thou shalt not borrow. And the Lord shall make thee the
head, and not the tail; and thou shalt be above only, and
thou shalt not be beneath; if that thou hearken unto the
commandments of the Lord thy God, which I command
thee this day, to observe it and to do them (Deuteronomy
28:12-13 KJV).

Now you declare
I decree and declare that the Lord my God shall open
unto me his good treasure. In his season, he shall cause
heaven to rain on my land. I shall not be barren. I shall
not have dry land. I shall be the head and never the tail. I
shall be above only and not beneath. I am who God says
I am, and today I commit to his commandments so my
life will be beautiful. I know the truth, and I will allow it
to set me free.

Chapter 8: Declarations for Marriage

Kingdom truths concerning Marriage and Prayer Declarations

This book is about knowing the truth of God's word and living it to the fullest. The truth about marriage is that God first established it, and it is between a man and a woman. It is originally designed to be an intimate union between a husband and a wife. The word of God says in Genesis 2:18, "It is not good that man should be alone; I will make a helper comparable to him." I, therefore, believe there is a suitable mate for everyone who desires the marriage covenant. Marriage is one of the beautiful things amongst many others God created, and it is to be enjoyed not endured. The word, once again, clearly states, "Do not be unequally yoked together with unbelievers. For what fellowship has righteousness with unrighteousness?" (2 Corinthians 6:14 KJV) When we defy the commandments of God, we somehow suffer the consequences. I encourage you to know the truth of God's word with respect to marriage and godly union so you will remain fruitful and flourish. The ultimate purpose of a marriage union is to help reflect the relationship God has with his people. The Bible goes on to refer to us, his creation, as brides. As the bridegroom rejoices over the bride, so shall your God rejoice over you (Isaiah 62:5 KJV).

His word says...
So God created man in his own image, in the image of God he created him; male and female he created them.

And God blessed them. And God said to them, Be fruitful and multiply and fill the earth and subdue it and have dominion over the fish of the sea and over the birds of the heavens and over every living thing that moves on the earth (Genesis 1:27-28 KJV).

Now you declare
I decree and declare I am created in the full image of God, and so is my spouse. He has blessed us in all things and including our union. I confess today that we shall be fruitful, we shall multiply, we shall fill the earth, and we shall subdue it. The power to dominate has been given to us; therefore, we confess that we are winners and never losers. We shall succeed in our marriage, and the devil will have no place in us. We know the truth, and we will allow it to set us free.

His word says...
For thy Maker is thine husband; the Lord of hosts is his name; and thy Redeemer the Holy One of Israel; The God of the whole earth shall he be called (Isaiah 54:5 KJV).

Now you declare
I decree and declare this day that God is a good God. You have said in your word that you will never leave me nor forsake me. You instituted the marriage covenant. You know everything that pertains to my life and godliness. I will trust you forevermore because you hold my world in your hands. I know the truth, and I will allow it to set me free.

His word says...
Place me like a seal over your heart, like a seal on your arm. For love is as strong as death, its jealousy as enduring as the grave. Love flashes like fire, the brightest kind of flame. Many waters cannot quench love, nor can rivers drown it. If a man tried to buy love with all his wealth, his offer would be utterly scorned (Songs of Solomon 8:6-7 NLT).

Now you declare
I decree and declare that the Lord is a seal over my heart. The love I have for my partner is strong, and it flashes as fire. Nothing will quench my love, and I shall not compromise in any way to cause a wedge between us. God has put us together, and his spirit will remain with us and guide us all the way through. I know the truth, and I will allow it to set me free.

His word says...
This is my commandment: Love each other in the same way I have loved you. There is no greater love than to lay down one's life for one's friends (John 15:12-13 NLT).

Now you declare
I decree and declare that I will abide by God's commandments for my life. I make a commitment this day that I will love my spouse the same way God loves me. I will not allow anything to get in between us. I will make an effort daily to show affection and love, just as God has commanded. I know the truth, and I will allow it to set me free.

His word says...
Wherefore they are no more twain, but one flesh. What therefore God hath joined together, let not man put asunder (Matthew 19:6 KJV).

Now you declare
I decree and declare that my partner and I are one. I come against any individualistic spirit that may prevail amongst us. I proclaim longevity over this relationship and destroy any anti-marriage forces that will try to put us asunder. For the Lord, God put us together, and nothing shall separate us. I know the truth, and I will allow it to set me free.

Chapter 9: Declarations for Health

Kingdom truths concerning Health and Prayer Declarations

The God of all flesh who created us is perfect. His ultimate wish for us, his children, is to be in good health, have a sound mind, be physically equipped, and to live a good life. However, life changes and recent innovations have altered so much in man's life that God's initial plan for us is hard to witness on a daily basis. Throughout Scripture, we discover that God gave strict guidelines to perfect health. When we abide by the rules, we will be in good health, and our soul will prosper. The manufacturer or creator of the human body knows what's best for it and what will keep it functioning perfectly well. He created a manual for us to comply with–the Bible--just us any other manufacturer does have a guide. Our neglect of his manual gives the enemy access to afflict our bodies. We end up being stressed, our mind not in the right place. We need to follow God's principles to experience perfect health. The thief cometh not, but for to steal, and to kill, and to destroy: I am come that they might have life, and that they might have it more abundantly (John 10:10 KJV).

His word says...
Beloved, I wish above all things that thou mayest prosper and be in health, even as thy soul prospereth (3 John 1:2 KJV).

Now you declare
I decree and declare divine healing over my life today. I arrest every lie the enemy has sold me concerning my health. My father's wishes and plans for me are great. He wishes that I prosper, be in great health, and my soul prospers. I renew my mind with the blood of Jesus and walk in the promises of God for my life. I know the truth, and I will allow it to set me free.

His word says...
Behold, I will bring it health and cure, and I will cure them, and will reveal unto them the abundance of peace and truth (Jeremiah 33:6 KJV).

Now you declare
I decree and declare today that I am not helpless. Every infirmity, weakness, disease, and attack are all destroyed because God has brought me a cure! I declare peace over every area of my life! I am made whole and no longer under the grip and power of the evil one. Every assignment against my health is terminated today and forever. I know the truth, and I will allow it to set me free.

His word says...
But he was wounded for our transgressions, he was bruised for our iniquities: the chastisement of our peace was upon him; and with his stripes we are healed (Isaiah 53:5 KJV).

Now you declare

I decree and declare that my healing is already secured. Jesus Christ has paid the price for my total liberation. His sacrifice on the Cross, shed blood, and the stripes received on his body were all for my healing. I will not allow that to go waste. I know the truth, and I will allow it to set me free.

His word says...
He healeth the broken in heart, and bindeth up their wounds (Psalms 147:3 KJV).

Now you declare
I decree and declare I have safety in the Lord. I will rise above every disheartening situation in my life, for my father promises to comfort me and heal me where I hurt, especially my heart. I will not allow pain to gain roots to destroy me. I turn my life over to God, for he holds my world in his hands. Lord bind up every wound I have with your miraculous touch. I know the truth, and I will allow it to set me free.

His word says...
And Jesus went about all the cities and villages, teaching in their synagogues, and preaching the gospel of the kingdom, and healing every sickness and every disease among the people (Matthew 9:35 KJV).

Now you declare
I decree and declare that my father in heaven cares for

me. You wish above all things that your children prosper and be in good health. You are Lord over every sickness and infirmity. Nothing that will devastate my body can stand your wrath and power. I will enjoy the finished work of Christ in my life. Devil, you are defeated. I know the truth, and I will allow it to set me free.

Chapter 10: Declarations for Career/Business

Kingdom truths concerning Career/Business and Prayer Declarations

One aspect of life's decisions that comes with a lot of struggle is choosing the right career path or knowing what God has predestined for your life. Most times, as Christians, we have the desire to do things that are pleasing to our Heavenly Father, so we end up fasting, praying, and seeking the face of God for direction as to what path to take.

The question is, how does one hear from God? How can one tell he is in the details of what you are embarking? Many pray without using God's word as a reference or do not even know or read to discover what he is saying about their situation. God's way is perfect. All the Lord's promises prove true. He is a shield for all who look to him for protection (2 Samuel 22:31 (NLT). Come unto me, all ye that labour and are heavy laden, and I will give you rest (Matthew 11:28 KJV). All this is to say that our God did not intend to make life difficult for his children. Total reliance on him allows him to steer our lives in the best way it should go.

His word says...
Thou shalt make thy prayer unto him, and he shall hear thee, and thou shalt pay thy vows. Thou shalt also decree a thing, and it shall be established unto thee: and the light shall shine upon thy ways (Job 22:27-28 KJV).

Now you declare
I decree and declare that I shall not be anxious about anything. I will make my prayers daily to my Heavenly Father and pay all vows. He has put power in my mouth to speak things into divine existence. Therefore, I declare that I am successful, I am above, and not beneath, I am the head, and not the tail. I have favor with all men, and I shall lack nothing, in Jesus name. I know the truth, and I will allow it to set me free.

His word says...
Sow your seed in the morning and do not be idle with your hands in the evening, for you do not know whether morning or evening planting will succeed, whether this or that, or whether both alike will be good (Ecclesiastic 11:6 AMP).

Now you declare
I decree and declare I shall be diligent with my assignment. I shall not be discouraged by any means, but speak strength every day over my life to continue to work. For, very soon, I shall reap the benefits of my hard work. I am a child of God, and blessings are inevitable to me. I am a winner, and never and looser. I will prosper in all my endeavors, in Jesus name. I know the truth, and I will allow it to set me free.

His word says...
Commit your works to the LORD [submit and trust them to Him], And your plans will succeed [if you respond to His will and guidance] (Proverbs 16:3 AMP).
Now you declare

I decree and declare today that I will commit every career or business endeavor I am working on to the Lord. He sees what I cannot see, he knows what I do not know, he can handle things that are way above me, and I will not be stressed and frustrated anymore due to disobedience. I trust my Lord, and I am very certain of great success. His guidance is never faulty. I know the truth, and I will allow it to set me free.

His word says...
Thus saith the Lord, thy Redeemer, the Holy One of Israel; I am the Lord thy God which teacheth thee to profit, which leadeth thee by the way that thou shouldest go (Isaiah 48:17 KJV).

Now you declare
I decree and declare I have a perfect teacher. He is the Lord most high. I will submit this day to his teachings, and I am confident that I will not fail. I will enjoy profit every day. My teacher will direct my path and will show me great business and career strategies. He will not permit me to make unfruitful or unwise decisions because he cares about me. I yield myself totally to him today and forever. I know the truth, and I will allow it to set me free.

His word says...
If you need wisdom, ask our generous God, and he will give it to you. He will not rebuke you for asking. But when you ask him, be sure that your faith is in God alone. Do not waver, for a person with divided loyalty is as unsettled as a wave of the sea that is blown and tossed

by the wind. Such people should not expect to receive anything from the Lord. (James 1:5-7 NLT).

Now you declare
I decree and declare today that I need wisdom—divine wisdom! I humble myself and ask of him anything I need because he will freely give to me what I desire. I pray that my faith will increase, I will not waver, and I will not be double-minded but will remain focused and steadfast, looking up to God, the author, and finisher of my faith. I will not forfeit my blessings through doubt and unbelief. My Father is not a man that he should lie; neither is he the son of man that he should repent. Has he declared, and will he not do it? Nothing is impossible with Him. I know the truth, and I will allow it to set me free.

Chapter 11: Declarations for Ministry

Kingdom truths concerning Ministry and Prayer Declarations

Just like a career, the ministry is another area in life that many people struggle to decide and settle on. It is something that one cannot treat lightly or enter into without proper counsel and hearing the voice of God. The call to ministry, which requires dedication to God's work, is not a money-seeking venture. But rather, its focus is a passion for lost souls, shaping peoples' destinies, and redirecting them to their Heavenly Father. It is a great responsibility. Ministry work causes many to see you in a different light and makes them have high expectations of you. You become the Public Relations (PR) Officer for God to put it short, and you must represent him well. It comes with pain, rejection, stress, lots of prayers, and more, and when you say yes, you must be ready for the challenge. If it is truly God who wants your hands in the plow, then he will be there every step of the way. You will not need to depend on your strength and ability. He will see you through the journey.

His word says...
But as for you, continue in what you have learned and have become convinced of, because you know those from whom you learned it, and how from infancy you have known the Holy Scriptures, which are able to make you wise for salvation through faith in Christ Jesus. (2 Timothy 2: 14-15 NIV)

Now you declare
I decree and declare this day that the word of God will not depart from me. I will meditate on it daily and will keep reminding God's people of His word. I will not hesitate to bring correction to those who quarrel about God's words. The word of God is true and powerful, and I will not be ashamed to enforce the truth in His word to many that falter. I will this day avoid and not be engaged in unfruitful chatter, so I do not get my spirit contaminated. I make a decision to walk away from anything that will not bring glory to God. I will honor my God this day and forever. I know the truth, and I will allow it to set me free.

His Word says...
To the church of God in Corinth, to those sanctified (set apart, made holy) in Christ Jesus, who are selected and called as saints (God's people), together with all those who in every place call on and honor the name of our Lord Jesus Christ, their Lord and ours (1 Corinthians 1:2 AMP).

Now you declare
I decree and declare today that I am sanctified, and set apart in Christ Jesus for the work of the kingdom. From this day forth, I make a decision to be morally pure, separated from evil, and stay spiritually whole. I will honor the name of the Lord daily. I have been called by God to be his holy saint. He made me holy by means of Christ Jesus, just as he did for all people everywhere who call on the name of our Lord Jesus Christ, their Lord and ours. I know the truth, and I will allow it to set

me free.

His word says...
But Moses protested to God, "Who am I to appear before Pharaoh? Who am I to lead the people of Israel out of Egypt?" (Exodus 3:11 NLT)

Now you declare
I decree and declare today that I know who I am. I am the called of God. He has chosen me, set me apart, and sanctified me for His good works. My Father knows me better than I know myself. He has empowered and equipped me for His work. He will not give me anything that I cannot handle. I will trust Him all the way through, and I am confident that I can lead Gods people on the path He has laid out for them. I know the truth, and I will allow it to set me free.

His word says...
"But Lord," Gideon replied, "how can I rescue Israel? My clan is the weakest in the whole tribe of Manasseh, and I am the least in my entire family!" The Lord said to him, "I will be with you. And you will destroy the Midianites as if you were fighting against one man." Gideon replied, "If you are truly going to help me, show me a sign to prove that it is really the Lord speaking to me." (Judges 6:15 NLT)

Now You Declare
I decree and declare that I know who I am. I am a child of the Most High God. I was created in his image and likeness: My Father did not put fear, weakness, timidity,

or shyness in me. Therefore, in the name of Jesus, I rebuke anything that my Father in heaven did not plant in me. I am strong, powerful, and fearfully and wonderfully made to bring him glory. I can do whatever he says I can do. His spirit lives in me; therefore, my mortal body shall be quickened. I will be empowered to fulfill every assignment he has laid out for me to advance the kingdom. It shall not be by my might nor by my power but by the Spirit of the Lord. I know the truth, and I will allow it to set me free.

Chapter 12: Declarations for Children

Kingdom truths concerning Children and Prayer Declarations

Children are a blessing from God, and anyone whose quiver is full of them is blessed. They are a part of God's creative agenda. Children are God-given gifts through which he honors families. Children are a heritage from the LORD, offspring a reward from him (Psalm 127:3 NIV).

God has entrusted his children to parents as stewards. Some expectations and responsibilities come with this territory. If there are challenges along the path of upbringing, all we need to do is to go to the giver of the gift and believe him for direction, guidance, and protection. Our Father will not give us anything unbearable. He always seeks to have a deeper relationship with us so we can be on the path of perfection just as he is perfect. Never despise your children for they are our heavenly reward.

His word says...
And he lifted up his eyes, and saw the women and the children; and said, Who are those with thee? And he said, The children which God hath graciously given thy servant (Genesis 33:5 KJV).

Now you declare
I decree and declare that God is faithful. He has put laughter in my mouth. I am not cursed but blessed and highly favored by God. My children are a great gift to

me. They are my heritage, my hope, and my pride. God saw it fit to make me a steward of this great blessing. I will not believe the lies of the enemy that I am not a great parent. The Lord who gave me these children will equip, guide, and teach me what to do to bring them up in the fear and admonishing of him. I cannot do it by my strength and might, but I will rely on the counsel of my Father, the giver of the gift, who blesses and adds no sorrow. My children will grow beautifully, and many shall call me blessed. I know the truth, and I will allow it to set me free.

His word says...
Honor your father and your mother, so that you may live long in the land the Lord your God is giving you (Exodus 20:12 NIV).

Now you declare
I decree and declare today that I will set the example of honoring my mother and father so my children will also emulate and honor me as they grow. I will teach them the right things to do as instructed by my Heavenly Father; so they will not depart from it. I will bring them up in the things of God so their foundation will be solidified. They will stand out among their peers and win many to God. It is my prayer today that my children will be lovers of Christ, will not walk in deception, and will not be swayed by the vices of this modern world. Lord, honor my request for my children as I dedicate them to you. I know the truth, and I will allow it to set me free.

His word says...
Impress them on your children. Talk about them when you sit at home and when you walk along the road, when you lie down and when you get up (Deuteronomy 6:7 NIV).

Now you declare
I decree and declare that as for me and my family, we will serve the Lord; for I am not ashamed of the gospel, because it is the power of God that brings salvation to everyone who believes. I will not be ignorant of the devices of the enemy. The enemy comes to steal, kill, and destroy. Jesus came to give us life and life abundantly. I will share my struggles with my children and will show them how God has been faithful to me. My children will serve God with me, they will understand why I fight for them, they will desire the word of the Lord, and they will have great passion for the things of God. None of my children will serve the devil. My God is awesome, and he will honor and fulfill his word in our lives. I know the truth, and I will allow it to set me free.

His word says ...
Keep his decrees and commands, which I am giving you today, so that it may go well with you and your children after you and that you may live long in the land the Lord your God gives you for all time. (Deuteronomy 4:40 KJV)

Now you declare
I decree and declare today that I will live in

righteousness. I will keep the decrees and commands of my God so it will be well with my children and me. So we will live long in the land the Lord gives us for all time. We will abhor evil and commit to his statutes. We will seek his face daily for strength and grace to go through each day. We will know the commandments of God, and we will live by his ordinances so it will be well with us all the days of our lives. I know the truth, and I will allow it to set me free.

His word says...
You have taught children and infants to tell of your strength, silencing your enemies and all who oppose you (Psalm 8:2 KJV).

Now you declare
I decree and declare that my children will be taught of the Lord. They will be different from all their friends. They will excel in every endeavor of their life. They will not be weak. They will be above only and not beneath. My children will know the word of God, and by it, they will silence our enemies and all who oppose us. The Lord God is our hope and our strength; he will not leave us nor forsake us. I know the truth, and I will allow it to set me free.

Conclusion

The word of God is power. That power is for confrontation. We fight an unseen enemy, and our fight is towards an enemy who is in full motion to desensitize us. The victory has already been given to us, but it is not on a silver platter, and we need to be proactive and engage the word of God in declarations to enforce our victory.

There is something written in the Scriptures concerning us, and it's time for us to go all out in search of what is written about us. It is by doing so that we can live a fulfilled life. If we don't come to terms and know what is written concerning us, we will be just living and not actually fulfilling purpose.

From time to time, we need to examine ourselves to know if we are in the will of God. We need to ask ourselves, "Is this what I am supposed to be doing? Is this how I am supposed to be thinking or living my life?" We can find our place in life by studying God's word and getting acquainted with his guidelines for living (See Appendix 1 and 2 for more on God's guidelines for living). When you discover the secret to a particular area of your life through his word, your spirit will leap. If you locate it and apply it to your life, God will do it for you. Having a bunch of keys does not give you automatic access. You must find the right key to deploy to access the right door.

If we're going to do everything our father has called us to fulfill in our families, churches, communities, finances, marriage, health, and ministry, we must eradicate negativity with God's truth daily. Search his word consistently on every challenging area of your life, and you will gain the upper hand over your enemy.

Appendix 1: THE TEN COMMANDMENTS – GIVEN TO MOSES BY GOD[1]

God from time past has always wanted his children to obey his voice and follow his instructions. One of the first inscriptions to the Israelites is the Ten Commandments, stating strongly things that they must refrain from doing as children of God. This Appendix is to bring to remembrance God's laws which are not outdated but still relevant in our walk with our father.

- *I am the Lord thy God, thou shalt not have any strange gods before Me."*

This commandment forbids idolatry, the worship of false gods and goddesses, and it excludes polytheism, the belief in many gods, insisting instead on monotheism, the belief in one God. This commandment forbids making golden calves, and worshipping statues of Caesar, for example.

- *"Thou shalt not take the name of the Lord thy God in vain."*

The faithful are required to honor the name of God. It makes sense that if you're to love God with all your

---

[1] Mike Bennett, "Who Wrote the 10 Commandments," Life and Hope, https://lifehopeandtruth.com/bible/10-commandments/the-ten-commandments/who-wrote-the-10-commandments/ (accessed August 12, 2019).

heart, soul, mind, and strength, then you're naturally to respect the name of God with equal passion and vigor.

- **"Remember to keep holy the Sabbath day."**

The Jewish celebration of Sabbath (Shabbat) begins at sundown on Friday evening and lasts until sundown on Saturday. Catholic, Protestant, and Orthodox Christians go to church on Sunday, treating it as the Lord's Day instead of Saturday to honor the day Christ rose from the dead.

- *"Honor thy father and mother."*

This commandment obliges the faithful to show respect for their parents — as children and adults. Children must obey their parents, and adults must respect and see to the care of their parents, when they become old and infirm.

- *"Thou shalt not kill."*

The better translation from the Hebrew would be "Thou shalt not murder" — a subtle distinction but an important one to the Church. Killing an innocent person is considered murder. Killing an unjust aggressor to preserve your own life is still killing, but it isn't considered murder or immoral.

- *"Thou shalt not commit adultery."*

The sixth and ninth commandments honor human sexuality. This commandment forbids the actual, physical act of having immoral sexual activity, specifically adultery, which is sex with someone else's spouse or a spouse cheating on their partner. This commandment also includes fornication, which is sex between unmarried people, prostitution, pornography, homosexual activity, masturbation, group sex, rape, incest, pedophilia, bestiality, and necrophilia.

- *"Thou shalt not steal."*

The seventh and tenth commandments focus on respecting and honoring the possessions of others. This commandment forbids the act of taking someone else's property. The Catholic Church believes that this commandment also denounces cheating people of their money or property, depriving workers of their just wage, or not giving employers a full day's work for a full day's pay. Embezzlement, fraud, tax evasion, and vandalism are all considered extensions of violations of the Seventh Commandment.

- *"Thou shalt not bear false witness against thy neighbor."*

The Eighth Commandment condemns lying. Because God is regarded as the author of all truth, the Church believes that humans are obligated to honor the truth. The most obvious way to fulfill this commandment is not to lie — intentionally deceive another by speaking a falsehood. So a good Catholic is who you want to buy a used car from.

- *"Thou shalt not covet thy neighbor's wife."*

The Ninth Commandment forbids the intentional desire and longing for immoral sexuality. To sin in the heart, Jesus says, is to lust after a woman or a man in your heart with the desire and will to have immoral sex with them. Just as human life is a gift from God and needs to be respected, defended, and protected, so, too, is human sexuality. Catholicism regards human sexuality as a divine gift, so it's considered sacred in the proper context — marriage.

- ***"Thou shalt not covet thy neighbor's goods."***
The Tenth Commandment forbids the wanting to or taking someone else's property. Along with the Seventh Commandment, this commandment condemns theft and the feelings of envy, greed, and jealousy in reaction to what other people have.

Appendix 2: THE EIGHT BEATITUDES OF JESUS

Jesus Christ gave us the Beatitudes. They had one simple lesson and meaning that would help us live a good life and lead us to everlasting life in heaven.

Taken from the Gospel of St. Matthew 5:3-10 KJV:

- Blessed are the poor in spirit, for theirs is the kingdom of heaven.

- Blessed are they who mourn, for they shall be comforted.

- Blessed are the meek, for they shall inherit the earth.

- Blessed are they who hunger and thirst for righteousness, for they shall be satisfied.

- Blessed are the merciful for they shall obtain mercy.

- Blessed are the pure of heart, for they shall see God.

- Blessed are the peacemakers, for they shall be called children of God.

- Blessed are they who are persecuted for the sake of righteousness, for theirs is the kingdom of heaven."

A closed mouth is a closed destiny. Make daily declarations based on God's word and see a complete turnaround.

About the Author

Lady Helena Barnes studied, married and started life in the United Kingdom. She relocated to the United States with her husband and their first son, Caleb, where they have been blessed with three more sons, Jesse, Aaron and Israel. She is the wife of Pastor Seth Barnes, Senior Pastor of Action Chapel Virginia (ACV).

She is a proud spiritual daughter of Bishop Kibby Otoo (Bishop of Action Chapel North America, under the direction of Archbishop Nicholas Duncan-Williams). She has been privileged to serve as the head of the women's ministry at Action Chapel Virginia. In that role, through her tireless dedication and service, God birthed the *I Love Me Mandate*.

Lady Helena has been a blessing to many pregnant women in the ministry through prayer support, serving as a spiritual midwife from the day of conception until delivery. She also heads a group of passionate intercessors at ACV women's ministry to bring to manifestation the promises of God for their lives and that of the church as a whole.

Lady Helena is an entrepreneur, Certified Image Consultant, an author (I Love Me Devotional), and is gifted with many talents and is a great blessing to the body of Christ. She is also a devoted Christian and does not compromise by any means her beliefs and her faith in God. Helena has a unique taste for fashion and anyone who comes into contact with her attests to the fact that she loves looking good and elegant at all times because she believes she is royalty, and all royals need to let their apparel speak as such.

The I Love Me Mandate

This book as well as the I Love Me Devotional was birthed from the *I Love Me* Movement.

I Love Me is a religious organization that helps redirect women's focus to their true identity. It guides them through practical day-to-day experiences using biblical principles and spiritual mentorship.

The *I Love Me* Vision:
- To reaffirm our identity, which is in Christ, to walk in our pre-ordained purpose and follow God's original blueprint for our lives.

Mission:
1. To help promote the sense of one's own value or worth as a person, build self-esteem, cultivate self-respect and be reminded that God doesn't make junk. Our divine purpose and assignment on earth should be our ultimate drive and hope that motivates us forward. Irrespective of life's challenges, we must not allow anything to devalue our self-worth.

2. To walk in the knowledge that we have the only validation we will ever need from Jesus himself.

3. To break the spirit of fear and limitation, and urge each other on to walk in confidence and boldness. The plan is to build each other up so that like Mary and Elizabeth, we can speak life to each other and cheer each other on to the finish line.

Goal:
- The goal is to deal with the root cause of self-rejection, which is often brought on by poor vision. People fail to see their God-given inner strength because they look at external features and other situations life may have thrown at them.

Objective:
- The objective for this movement is to reclaim the truth, to go on the offensive and regain the confidence that God originally deposited in us.

Outcome:
- The outcome is to live victorious every day, to celebrate 'Me', Us, 'The Woman'. You, too, are somebody—somebody worth the sacrifice of what was most precious to God—his only Son and once this truth sinks, God's opinion becomes the only one that really matters.

For more information, visit
www.ilovemebyhelena.com

Coming Soon

Journey to Purpose:

Finding My Rhythm as a Minister's Wife
A New Book Release by Lady Helena Barnes

It takes an extraordinary breed of woman to accept the mandate of a First Lady. Often misunderstood, we as first ladies find that our identities and our purpose are shaped by virtue of the men of God that we are married to. I pray that every reader understands that they are significant. Outside of being a wife and a first lady, your individual destiny was created by God since the very beginning of time to bring him glory. You are a co-laborer with him, in Christ. You have a unique assignment and it is time to discover what that is. The very essence of who you are has been predetermined. Nothing that besets you in life should ever be downplayed. It is just one piece of the puzzle leading you to purpose.

If you feel as though he is the one wearing the cloak and you have been relegated to the background, this book will be a blessing to you. If you are not sure how you fit into his calling, know that with time, you will witness the unfolding of your own destiny, just as I did. Some will find their purpose before they get married. Some will be joined together already fulfilling purpose, and for others, purpose unfolds with time. This book will help you to value endurance and travail through prayer in pursuit of your assignment as his partner, as a minister, and as a first lady.

www.ingramcontent.com/pod-product-compliance
Lightning Source LLC
LaVergne TN
LVHW051155080426
835508LV00021B/2638